CONTENTS

WHO WAS AMELIA EARHART?

Amelia Earhart was an American **pilot**. She was the first woman to fly **solo** across the Atlantic Ocean.

Amelia lived at a time when most women didn't even drive a car. People were amazed that she would dare to fly a plane.

Sadly, Amelia died when she was only 41 years old. Her plane **disappeared** when she was flying over the Pacific Ocean.

Amelia made her last flight in a plane like this. What make of plane did she fly on her last journey?

FACT CAT FACT

Planes were a new **invention** when Amelia was growing up. The first plane flight was in 1903 when Amelia was six years old.

YOUNG AMELIA

Amelia Earhart was born in 1897 in the state of Kansas, USA. Her family moved around a lot when she was a child and she didn't spend much time at school.

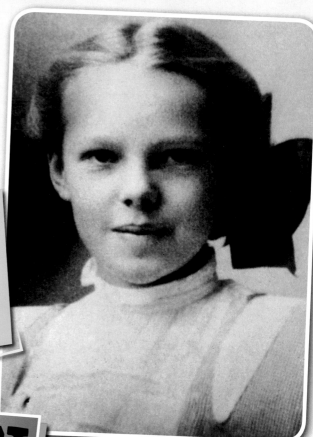

Amelia enjoyed reading books, but she **preferred** playing outside. She loved riding horses and climbing trees.

FACT CAT FACT

When Amelia was seven she went on a **roller coaster** ride. Back at home she built her own roller coaster from pieces of wood. She said riding on it felt like flying!

At the age of 20, Amelia moved to Canada. She worked as a nurse, looking after soldiers who had been **wounded** in **World War One**.

This photograph shows a nurse in World War One. Amelia worked as a nurse until the end of the war. What year did World War One end?

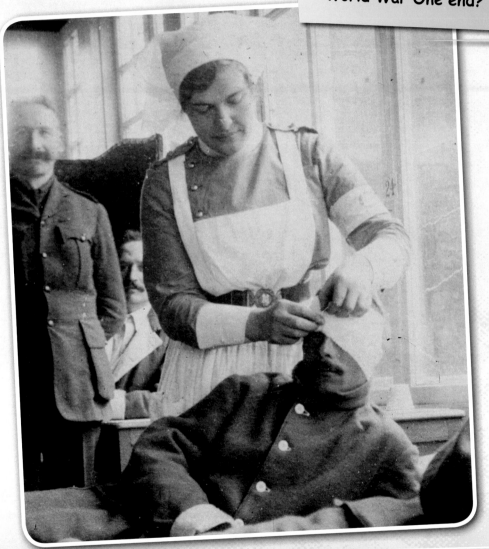

LEARNING TO FLY

After the war, Amelia decided she wanted to be a pilot. But first she needed to know how planes worked. Her first step was to learn about motor cars.

This is what cars looked like when Amelia was young. She went to classes to learn to repair cars when they **broke down**.

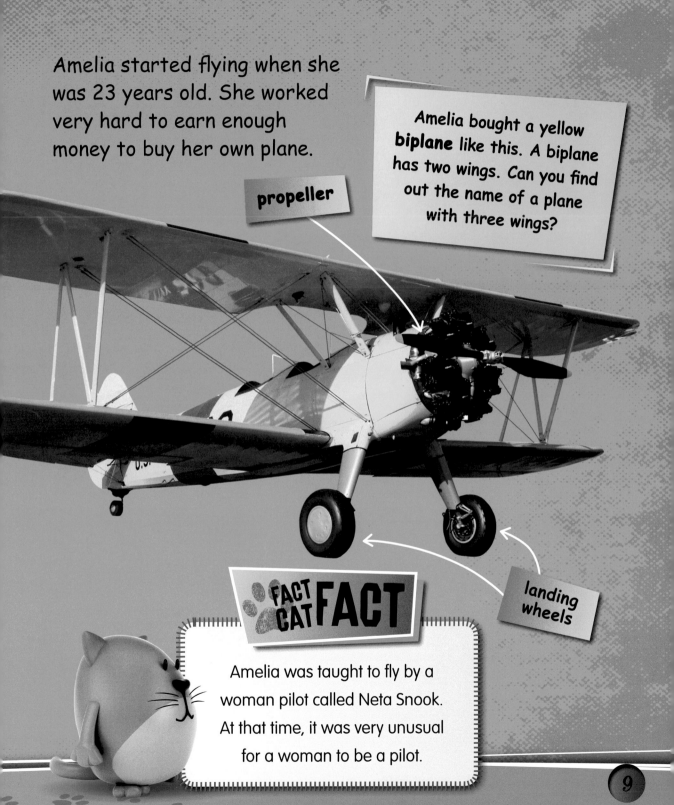

Amelia started flying when she was 23 years old. She worked very hard to earn enough money to buy her own plane.

Amelia bought a yellow **biplane** like this. A biplane has two wings. Can you find out the name of a plane with three wings?

propeller

landing wheels

FACT CAT FACT

Amelia was taught to fly by a woman pilot called Neta Snook. At that time, it was very unusual for a woman to be a pilot.

FLYING ADVENTURES

When she was 27, Amelia moved to Boston, USA. She found a job as a **social worker**, helping poor families. She went flying whenever she could, and she became a very **skilful** pilot.

Amelia took part in air shows, where pilots showed off their skills. They performed **daring** tricks, such as flying very close together.

Charles
Lindbergh

In the 1920s, some pilots began to make very long flights. Some of them even dared to fly across the sea.

In 1927, a pilot called Charles Lindbergh flew solo across the Atlantic Ocean. Can you find out the name of his plane?

NEW YORK

PARIS

FACT CAT FACT

Lindbergh's flight from New York to Paris lasted 33 hours and 30 minutes. Today, **passenger planes** make the same journey in less than eight hours.

ACROSS THE ATLANTIC

After Lindbergh's **transatlantic** flight, many people hoped that a woman would fly across the Atlantic Ocean. Amelia was chosen for this adventure. She flew with two male pilots in a plane called the *Friendship*.

The *Friendship* was a **seaplane**. It took off from the coast of Newfoundland. What country does the island of Newfoundland belong to?

On 17 June 1928 the *Friendship* left Newfoundland. Less than 21 hours later, it landed in South Wales.

The pilots were welcomed as heroes. Wilmer Stultz is on the left. Amelia is in the centre and Louis Gordon is on the right.

Amelia had never flown a seaplane, so she was not a pilot on the flight. She kept a **log**, writing down what happened on the journey.

FLYING SOLO

Amelia's transatlantic flight made her **famous**, even though she wasn't a pilot on the flight. She wrote a book and gave talks about flying. She also **modelled** clothes for **fashion** companies.

When she was 33, Amelia married George Putnam. George wanted Amelia to try new flying **challenges**.

In 1932 Amelia made a solo flight across the Atlantic Ocean. She flew from Newfoundland to Northern Ireland.

Amelia' flight took less than 15 hours. Can you find the date when her plane arrived in Ireland?

NORTHERN IRELAND

CANADA

Newfoundland

Paris

ATLANTIC OCEAN

N
W E
S

FACT CAT FACT

Amelia planned to land in Paris, but there were very strong winds so she decided to land in Northern Ireland.

NEW CHALLENGES

Amelia set many more flying **records**. She was the first person to fly solo from Hawaii to California. She was also the fastest woman pilot to fly across the USA.

In 1935, Amelia bought a new plane. It had all the latest **equipment**. This made it much easier for pilots to **navigate**.

Amelia planned to fly all the way round the world in her new plane! She asked Fred Noonan to be her **navigator**. He helped her plan a **route**, with stops to fill up the plane with **fuel**.

Amelia and Fred planned over 30 stops. How many stops does a modern passenger plane make when it flies from London to Sydney, Australia?

FACT CAT FACT

Amelia aimed to be the first woman to fly around the world. An American man called Wiley Post flew around the world in 1931.

FLYING ROUND THE WORLD

In March 1937, Amelia set off to fly round the world. She flew west from Oakland, California, and made her first stop on Hawaii. But her plane was damaged as it left Hawaii so she had to give up.

Amelia decided to try again, but this time she planned to fly east. This map shows the route she planned. Can you name the **continents** on her route?

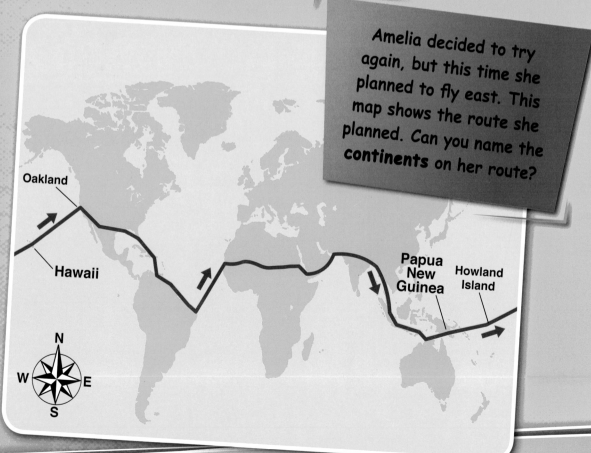

Oakland

Hawaii

Papua
New
Guinea

Howland
Island

N
W · E
S

Amelia left Oakland, California on 21 May, 1937. She followed the route she had planned until she reached Papua New Guinea.

On 2 July, Amelia and Fred left Papua New Guinea and headed for Howland Island. The island is very hard to spot from the air because it is only 3 kilometres (2 miles) wide.

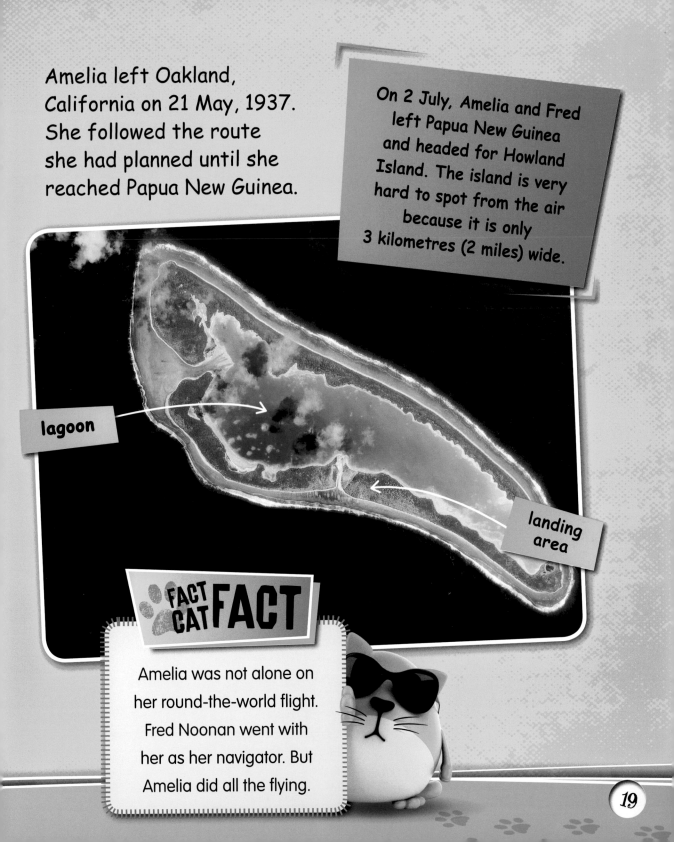

lagoon

landing area

FACT CAT FACT

Amelia was not alone on her round-the-world flight. Fred Noonan went with her as her navigator. But Amelia did all the flying.

AMELIA DISAPPEARS

Amelia sent radio messages as she flew over the Pacific Ocean. After six hours, she reported that she was 160 kilometres (100 miles) away from Howland Island.

In her next message, Amelia reported that her plane was running out of fuel. She also said she couldn't see the island. She sent one more message giving her position. Then there was silence.

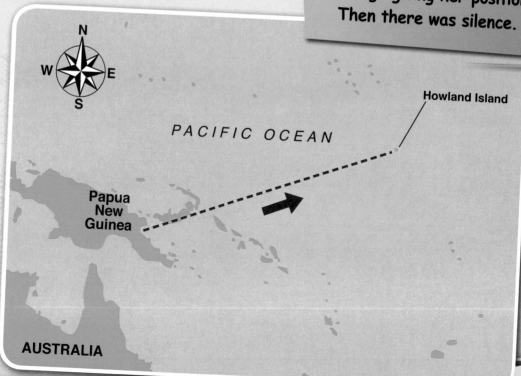

Howland Island

PACIFIC OCEAN

Papua New Guinea

AUSTRALIA

There was a massive search for Amelia and Fred. But they were never found. Most people believed that they had drowned.

Amelia has never been forgotten. There is an Amelia Earhart museum in the town where she was born. Can you find out where it is?

FACT CAT FACT

A few people believed that Amelia didn't drown. They said she had been captured by people who thought she was a **spy**.

Try to answer the questions below. Look back through the book to help you. Check your answers on page 24.

1 Amelia's plane disappeared over the Atlantic. True or not true?

a) true

b) not true

2 Amelia was a nurse in World War One. Where did she work?

a) The USA

b) France

c) Canada

3 Who was the first man to fly across the Atlantic?

a) Orville Wright

b) Charles Lindbergh

c) Fred Noonan

4 Amelia was the first person to fly solo from Hawaii to California. True or not true?

a) true

b) not true

5 What was the last place that Amelia stopped on her round the world flight?

a) Papua New Guinea

b) Hawaii

c) Howland Island

GLOSSARY

broke down stopped working

challenge something difficult to do

continent one of the seven large masses of land on the Earth. Europe, Asia and North America are all continents

daring very brave

disappear to vanish or to stop being seen

equipment the things someone needs to do a job

fashion a popular style of clothes

fuel petrol or gas that is burned to make a plane fly

invention a new machine that has been designed to do a job

lagoon a large pool of seawater

log a written record of something that has happened

model to show off clothes by wearing them

navigate to plan the route for a plane, ship or car

navigator someone who plans the route for a plane, ship or car

passenger plane a plane that carries people

pilot someone who controls a plane or a ship

position a place where something or someone can be found

prefer to like one thing better than another thing

propeller a set of blades that spin around very fast and produce the power to drive a plane through the air

record the fastest or the first way of doing something

repair to mend something

roller coaster a fairground ride in which a set of carts run on rails with many steep slopes

route the way to get from one place to another

seaplane an aircraft with floats that lands on water and takes off from water

social worker someone who offers help to people who have problems

solo alone

spy someone who secretly collects information about an enemy

transatlantic across the Atlantic Ocean

World War One the major war that was fought between 1914 and 1918

wounded cut or hurt

INDEX

ANSWERS

Pages 5–21

page 5: Amelia made her last flight in a Lockheed Model 10 Electra.

page 7: World War One ended in 1918.

page 9: A plane with three wings is called a triplane.

page 11: Lindbergh's plane was called the *Spirit of St Louis*.

page 12: The island of Newfoundland belongs to Canada.

page 15: Amelia's plane arrived in Northern Ireland on May 21, 1932.

page 17: A modern passenger plane usually makes one stop on a flight from London to Sydney.

page 18: Amelia flew over North America, South America, Africa, Asia and Australia.

page 21: The Amelia Earhart Birthplace Museum is in Atchison, Kansas, USA.

Quiz answers

1   b) not true. Amelia's plane disappeared over the Pacific Ocean.

2   c) Amelia worked as a nurse in Canada.

3   b) Charles Lindbergh

4   a) true

5   a) Papua New Guinea